SPACE ENCYCLOPEDIA

# THE MILKY WAY

An imprint of Om Books International

# Contents

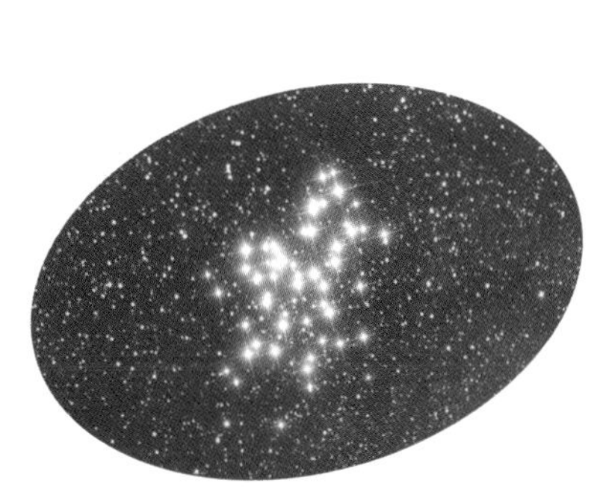

# The Milky Way

▲ *Spiral galaxy NGC 6744 is believed to resemble the Milky Way a lot.*

The Milky Way was formed shortly after the Big Bang as one of the denser areas of mass distribution in the universe. Compare this to a pudding with lumps in it, the lumps being the stuff the universe emerged from. Some of these denser areas were globular clusters, which contain older stars.

These stars form the stellar halo. Within a few billion years of the formation of the first stars, the Milky Way had accumulated so much mass that it started spinning quickly. Due to the conservation of the amount of rotation, the gaseous interstellar medium collapsed from a near-spherical shape and changed to a flat disc. Thus, the newer stars, including the Sun, formed in this spiral disc.

The galaxy formation process has not stopped as our universe is constantly evolving. The Milky Way has already swallowed several galaxies and is expected to collide with the nearest galaxy Andromeda in a few billion years.

# Parts of the Milky Way

The Milky Way consists of three basic components: (1) the disc that contains the spiral arms, (2) the halo and (3) the nucleus or the central bulge. The halo and the nucleus are collectively referred to as the spherical components of the galaxy.

### Bulge

The bulge is a round structure made primarily of old stars, gas and dust. The outer parts of the bulge are difficult to distinguish from the halo. This bulge of the Milky Way is about 10,000 light years across.

### Halo

It primarily contains single old stars and clusters of old stars. It also contains dark matter, which is the material that we cannot see. The Milky Way's halo may be over 130,000 light years across.

### Disc

The disc is a flattened region that covers the bulge in a spiral galaxy. It is shaped like a pancake. The Milky Way's disc is 100,000 light years across and 1,000 light years thick. It consists of mostly young stars, gas and dust, which are concentrated in its spiral arms. Some old stars are also present.

### Spiral arms

The spiral arms are curved extensions. They begin at the bulge of a spiral galaxy, appearing like a "pinwheel". The spiral arms contain a lot of gas and dust, as well as young blue stars. They are found only in spiral galaxies.

### Stars, gas and dust

There are different types of stars. The blue stars for example are very hot and usually have a shorter lifespan as compared to the cool red stars. The regions of galaxies where stars are currently forming are bluer than the regions where there has been no recent star formation. Spiral galaxies have a lot of gas and dust, whereas elliptical galaxies contain very little of it.

# Centre of the Milky Way

The galactic centre is the rotational centre of the Milky Way. It is located about 27,000 light years from Earth. There is believed to be a supermassive black hole (SBMH) at the centre of the Milky Way, known as Sagittarius A* (Sgr A*). Besides the Sgr A*, there are massive star clusters, such as the Arches, Quintuplet and the GC star cluster.

## Supermassive black hole

An SMBH is the largest type of black hole, in the range of many hundreds of thousands to billions of solar masses. The SMBH is found in the centre of almost all massive galaxies.

## In and around the SMBH

The accretion of gas around the black hole, typically in the shape of a disc, works as a major fuel for the SMBH. The central region around the Sagittarius A* contains thousands of other stars. More than 100 OB and Wolf–Rayet stars have been identified by scientists so far. However, the existence of young stars is baffling to scientists. This is because black holes are supposed to emit tidal forces, which in turn should have prevented any star formation activities. But the young stars exist in spite of this.

*A vector of the supermassive black hole at the centre of the Milky Way.*

*Chandra X-ray observatory image of Sagittarius A*, the radio source corresponding to the SMBH of the Milky Way galaxy.*

## Sagittarius A*

It is a bright and very compact astronomical radio source at the centre of the Milky Way, near the border of the constellations Sagittarius and Scorpius. On the 13th and 15th of February, 1974, two astronomers Bruce Balick and Robert Brown discovered Sgr A*. They made use of the baseline interferometer of the National Radio Astronomy Observatory for their discovery. The name Sgr A* was coined by Brown because the radio source was "exciting", and excited states of atoms are denoted with asterisks.

**FUN FACT**

Did you know that Sagittarius A is a larger astronomical feature that comprises the Sagittarius A*?

# Spiral Staircase and the Arms of the Milky Way

There are three main types of galaxies: ellipticals, spirals and irregulars. This classification is based on the shape of the galaxy. The spiral-type galaxies have spiral arms that are similar to the shape of a spiral staircase. The spiral structure has been a mystery to astrophysicists since many years. The most common theory today is that a spiral structure can be regarded as a density wave, which revolves in the galactic disc like waves spread in the ocean.

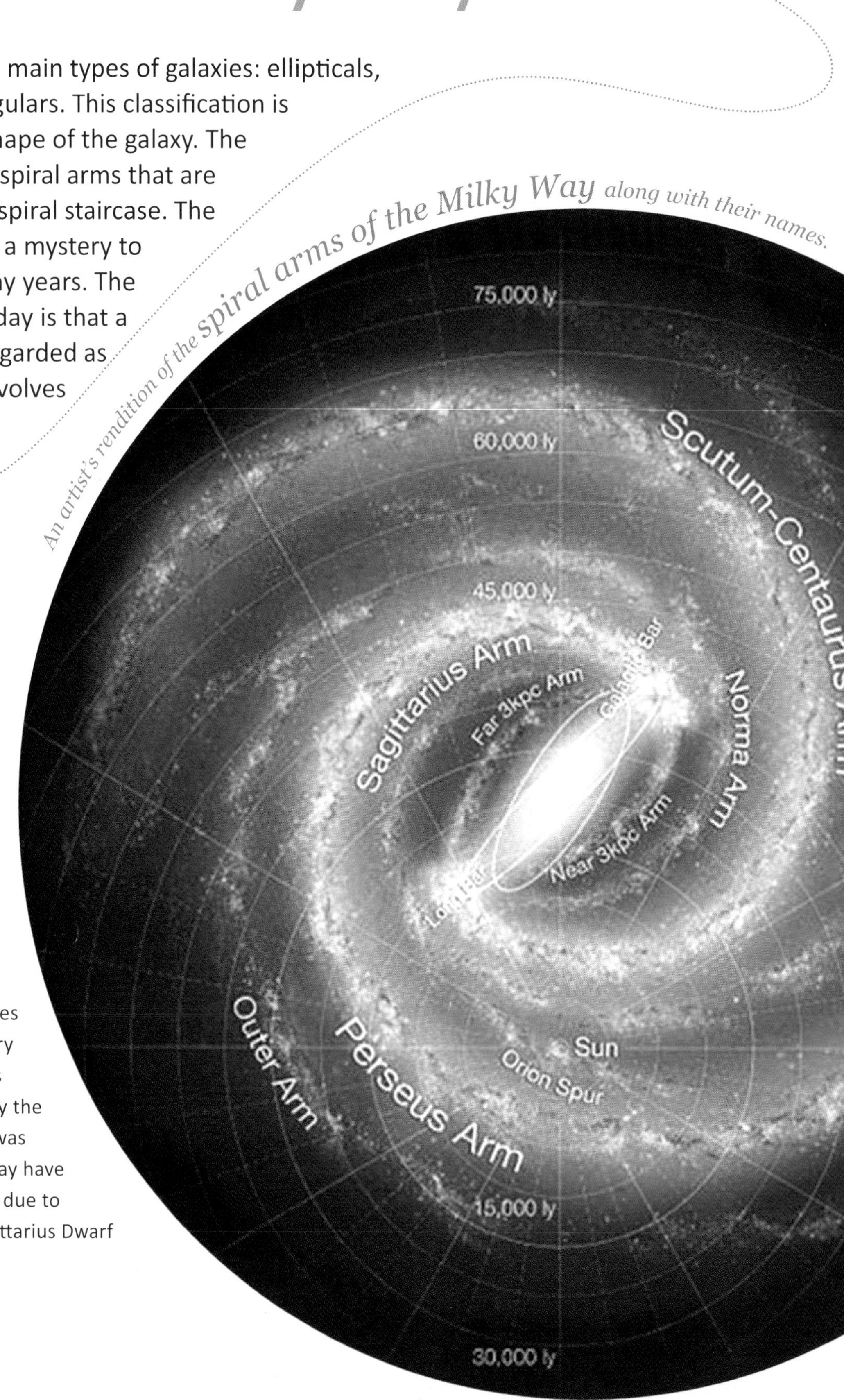


An artist's rendition of the spiral arms of the Milky Way along with their names.

## Movement of arms

Like stars, the spiral arms also rotate around the centre, but unlike the stars, they do so with constant angular velocity, which means that stars pass in and out of spiral arms.

As the gas in the interstellar medium passes into the density wave, it becomes denser, and this leads to the formation of new stars. The hottest and brightest stars have short lifetimes so that they are born and die very close to the density wave. This is why the spiral arms are traced by the brightest and youngest stars. It was suggested that the Milky Way may have obtained its spiral arm structure due to repeated collisions with the Sagittarius Dwarf Elliptical galaxy.

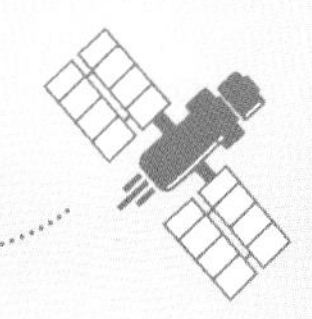

## Formation of arms

Our Milky Way is a barred as well as a spiral galaxy. This means that our galaxy probably has two major spiral arms, plus a central bar. However, there is also the possibility that our galaxy contains four arms or there may be only two arms, or our galaxy could even have two main arms and two extra arms. This point is still being debated and a conclusion is yet to be reached. The spiral arms are named after the location in which we view them in the sky, which is given as follows:

- Perseus arm (considered one of the two primary spiral arms)
- Outer arm or Norma
- Scutum–Centaurus arm (considered as one of the two primary spiral arms)
- Carina–Sagittarius arm
- Orion–Cygnus arm/Orion spur (which contains the Sun and our solar system)

### Description of the arms

The Perseus arm is the arm that is just outside the Sun's location in the galaxy. It is about 700–1000 parsecs from us. Beyond the Perseus arm, there may be a more distant arm, but they become less distinct in the outer galaxy zone. On the inside of the Sun's orbit lies the Sagittarius–Scutum arm. On the inside of the Sagittarius–Scutum arm, we can find the Centaurus–Carina arm. This is at a distance of approximately 3000 parsecs from the centre.

### Spiral patterns

It is thought that the Milky Way contains two different spiral patterns. The first one is the inner one. This is formed by the Sagittarius arm, which is the one that rotates fast. The second one is the outer one, formed by the Carina and Perseus arms, which has a rotation velocity, which is slower and whose arms are also tightly wound.

## Sun's location in our galaxy

Surprisingly, we're not located in one of the Milky Way's two primary spiral arms. Contrary to popular belief, our solar system is actually located in one of the minor arms. The arm that we are located in is called the Orion arm or the Orion spur. The Orion spur lies between the Perseus arm and the Carina–Sagittarius arm of the Milky Way.

The Sun is located at a distance that is nearly two-thirds of the radius of the disc from its centre. The Orion spur merges with the Perseus spiral arm towards the constellation named Cygnus.

## Importance of spiral arms

Besides being the primary sites of star formation, the spiral arms are important in determining many factors within the galaxy. These factors include the density, temperature and chemical composition (i.e., the amount of carbon, hydrogen, oxygen, etc.) of the interstellar gas, as well as the dynamics of the stars and the gases within the galaxy.

*A barred, spiral galaxy, like our Milky Way.*

**FUN FACT**

According to studies, as spirals burn through their gas and dust and their star formation decreases, they lose their spiral shape and move on to the next stage of galactic evolution—elliptical galaxies.

# Milky Way's Halo

The galactic disc of the Milky Way is surrounded by a spheroidal halo of old stars and globular clusters, most of which lie within 100,000 light years of the galactic centre. Globular clusters date back to 15 billion years and are the oldest components of the galaxy.

## Constituents of the halo

The halo is spherical in shape and contains a little gas, dust or star formation. It extends beyond the disc.

The clusters found in the halo are globular clusters and therefore, are stellar remnants, low mass stars or other low mass objects. Halo stars are not the first generation of stars because they contain elements heavier than hydrogen and helium.

The halo stars pass through the disc and the nucleus of the galaxy, but spend the majority of their time far above or below the plane of the galaxy.

## Gaseous halo

In addition to the stellar halo, there is a gaseous halo with a large amount of hot gas. The halo extends for hundreds of thousands of light years, much further than the stellar halo and close to the distance of the Large and Small Magellanic Clouds. This hot halo has a mass that is almost equal to the mass of the Milky Way. The temperature of this halo gas ranges from 1 million to 2.5 million K.

## Accumulation of stars

Halo stars could have been acquired from small galaxies, that fall into and merge with the spiral galaxy. The Sagittarius Dwarf Spheroidal galaxy, for example, is in the course of merging with the Milky Way. Observations show that some stars in the halo of the Milky Way have been acquired from it.

### FUN FACT

Did you know that the swirling gases around a black hole transform it into an electrical generator, making it spout jets of electricity billions of kilometres into space?

# Beyond the Milky Way

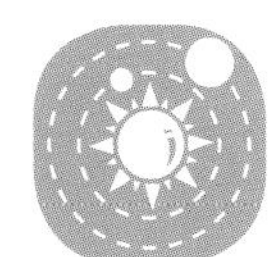

"Who are we? We find that we live on an insignificant planet of a humdrum star lost in a galaxy tucked away in some forgotten corner of a universe in which there are far more galaxies than people". – Carl Sagan

*One could say that our sky is a window to the universe. In the image above, everything we can see is a part of our Milky Way galaxy. It is vast, beautiful and full of hundreds of billions of stars, planets, and much, much more.*

## The wonders of our galaxy

If one is to look beyond our galaxy with current telescopes, astronomers have observed middle-aged and mature galaxies. Using the Hubble Space Telescope provided the most detailed view of the early universe. Almost 1500 galaxies were observed at various stages of evolution, some even old enough to date back to when the universe was only a billion years old.

*Coddington's nebula is a dwarf irregular galaxy in Ursa Major.*

## Strange objects in space

Many recognisable shapes were seen in space, which appear red due to the light emitted from older, mature stars. For example, the crystal blue spiral galaxies that are brilliantly illuminated by virtue of the glow of their hot, young stars. Amongst these, also noted were strange, tadpole-like objects that were apparently merging galaxies, also known as "train wrecks". In addition, multiple faint dwarf galaxies were observed.

## What is missing?

We need more information on how far away these galaxies are from us, how these galaxies cluster and clump together, how quickly they're moving either towards, or away from both us and each other, and how massive they really are.

Certain objects may even date back to the first generation of stars and galaxies. Is it possible that some of these cosmic shards and fragments evolved into the galaxies we recognise today? Could it be that they are actually small but appear bright because of great bursts of star formation? They could be massive, with most of their stellar population hidden by dust clouds.

# Galactic Neighbours

Our Milky Way galaxy is not alone in its cosmic neighbourhood. It belongs to the Local Group, which is a set of about 50 galaxies that are united due their reciprocal gravitational attraction. The Local Group is dominated by two massive galaxies: the Milky Way and Andromeda galaxies, a close analogue of our galaxy that is about 2.5 million light years away. Let's take a look at our closest galactic neighbours.

### 1. Andromeda

Most people believe that the Andromeda galaxy is our closest neighbour. However, Andromeda is the closest spiral galaxy and not the closest galaxy.

*The Large Magellanic Cloud is recognised as a disrupted barred spiral galaxy.*

### 3. Large Magellanic Cloud

The Large Magellanic Cloud (LMC) is a nearby galaxy, and a satellite of the Milky Way.

*This is a real image of M31 "Andromeda galaxy" taken with a 10-inch astrograph telescope.*

### 2. Triangulum

It is a spiral galaxy approximately three million light years from Earth in the constellation Triangulum.

*This is sometimes informally referred to as the Pinwheel galaxy.*

**FUN FACT**

Did you know that if you fell into a black hole, you would stretch like spaghetti?

*Star formation in NGC 602, a part of the wing region of the Small Magellanic Cloud. Magellanic Clouds have long been included in the folklore of native inhabitants of south sea islanders and indigenous Australians.*

## 5. Barnard's galaxy

Barnard's galaxy, also known as NGC 6822, IC 4895 or Caldwell 57, is a barred irregular galaxy approximately 1.6 million light years away in the constellation Sagittarius.

*Palomar 12 was first suspected to have been captured from the Sagittarius dwarf galaxy about 1.7 Ga ago in 2000.*

## 7. Sagittarius Dwarf

The Sagittarius Dwarf elliptical galaxy is a small, elliptical, loop-shaped, satellite galaxy of our Milky Way that lies about 70,000 light years away from Earth in the constellation of Sagittarius.

## 4. Small Magellanic Cloud

The Small Magellanic Cloud (SMC) is one of our closest neighbours.

*This dwarf galaxy is about a tenth of the Milky Way's size and contains only 10 million stars.*

## 6. Sextans A

Also known as UGCA 205, it is a tiny dwarf irregular galaxy. It spans about 5000 light years across.

*Irregular galaxy Sextans A.*

# Andromeda

The Andromeda galaxy (M31) is a spiral galaxy that is approximately 2.5 million light years from Earth in the Andromeda constellation. It is the nearest spiral galaxy to Milky Way. It gets its name from the area of the sky in which it appears in the Andromeda constellation and is the largest galaxy in the Local Group.

## Star formation

M31 was formed out of the collision of two smaller galaxies between five and nine billion years ago. According to scientists, Andromeda was born roughly 10 billion years ago from the merger of many smaller proto-galaxies. The rate at which stars form within the Milky Way is much higher. M31 produces roughly around one solar mass per year as compared to the three to five solar masses of the Milky Way. The rate of supernovae in the Milky Way is also twice that of M31. M31 contains one trillion ($10^{12}$) stars, at least twice the number of stars in the Milky Way galaxy.

## Barred spiral galaxy

The galaxy is a barred spiral galaxy, with the Andromeda galaxy's bar viewed almost directly along its long axis. The spiral arms are outlined by a series of H II regions, described as resembling "beads on a string". Studies show two spiral arms that appear to be tightly wound, although they are more widely spaced than in our galaxy.

## Andromeda's nucleus

M31 is known to harbour a dense and compact star cluster at its very centre. The luminosity of the nucleus is in excess of the most luminous globular clusters.

There are approximately 460 globular clusters associated with the Andromeda galaxy. The most massive of these clusters, Globular One, has the greatest luminosity in the Local Group with several million stars.

## Satellites

The Andromeda galaxy has satellite galaxies, consisting of 14 known dwarf galaxies. The best known and readily observed satellite galaxies are M32 and M110.

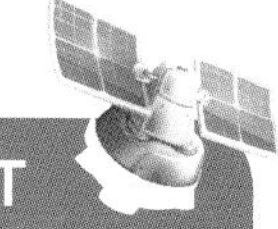

**FUN FACT**

**The Andromeda and Milky Way are about 2.5 million light years apart. Fuelled by gravity, the two galaxies are hurtling towards one another at a speed of 402,000 km per hour!**

*The Andromeda galaxy.*

# Andromeda–Milky Way Collision

A galactic collision, the Andromeda–Milky Way collision, is predicted to occur in about 4 billion years. It will be between the Milky Way and the Andromeda galaxies, the two largest galaxies in the Local Group.

A representation of Earth in the Milky Way and Andromeda approaching it.

## Stellar collisions

While the Andromeda galaxy contains about one trillion stars and the Milky Way contains about 300 billion, the chance of even two stars colliding is negligible because of the huge distances between the stars.

## Black hole collisions

The Milky Way and Andromeda galaxies each contain a central supermassive black hole that will converge near the centre of the newly formed galaxy. When they come within one light year of one another, they will emit gravitational waves that will radiate further orbital energy until they completely merge. Gas taken up by the combined black hole will likely create a luminous quasar or an active galactic nucleus.

## Fate of the solar system

Based on current calculations, scientists predict a 50 per cent chance that in a merged galaxy the solar system will be swept out three times farther from the galactic core than its current distance. There's also a 12 per cent chance that the solar system will be ejected from the new galaxy sometime during the collision. However, there would be no adverse effect on the system and the chances of any disturbance to the Sun or planets may be unlikely. Without intervention, by the time the two galaxies collide, the surface of Earth will have already become far too hot for liquid water to exist, thereby ending all terrestrial life.

## Merger remnant

According to simulations, this post-collision object will look like a giant elliptical galaxy, but with fewer stars than the current elliptical galaxies. It is, however, possible that it could result in the formation of a large disc galaxy.

An artist's representation showing the collision of Andromeda and Milky Way.

**FUN FACT**

It is predicted that in a few billion years, the Milky Way galaxy will collide with the Andromeda galaxy to form one super galaxy.

# Large Magellanic Cloud

A galaxy close by is the Large Magellanic Cloud (LMC). It is also a satellite of the Milky Way. At a distance of slightly less than approximately 157,000 light years, it is the third closest galaxy to the Milky Way. This dwarf galaxy can be seen like a faint cloud in the sky in the Southern Hemisphere. It is located on the border of the two constellations – Dorado and Mensa.

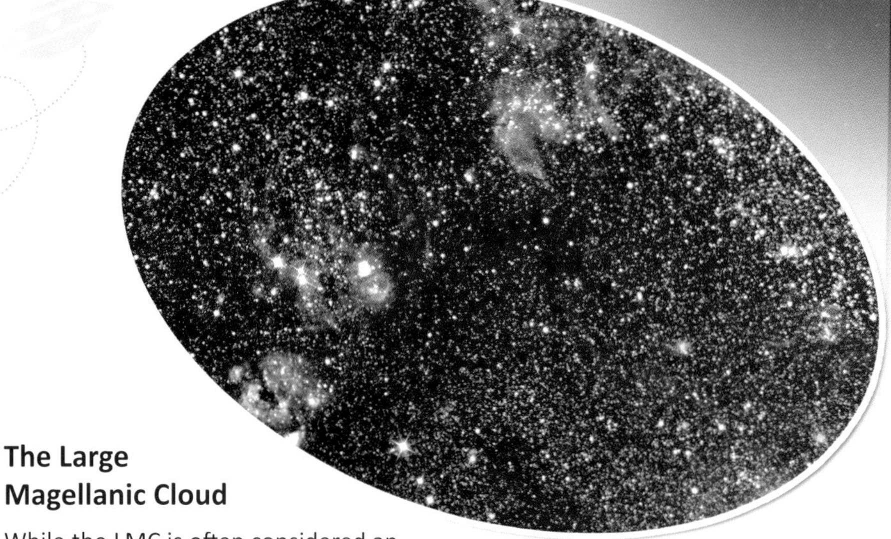

*Tarantula Nebula, in LMC, the most active star-forming region in the Local Group.*

## The Large Magellanic Cloud

While the LMC is often considered an irregular-type galaxy, the LMC has a prominent central bar and spiral arm. The central bar seems to be warped so that the east and west ends are closer to the Milky Way than the middle. The irregular appearance of the LMC's could be due to tidal interactions with the Milky Way and the SMC. The mass of LMC is equivalent to around 10 billion times the mass of the Sun (1010 solar masses). This makes it approximately 1/100th as massive as the Milky Way with a diameter of about 14,000 light years.

## Features of the LMC

Like many irregular galaxies, the LMC is rich in gas and dust, and it is currently undergoing vigorous star-formation activity. The LMC is full of a wide range of galactic objects and phenomena that make it aptly known as an "astronomical treasure-house" described by American astronomer Robert Burnham Jr.

Surveys carried out of the galaxy have revealed nearly 60 globular clusters, 700 open clusters and 400 planetary nebulae together with over thousands of giant and super giant stars. The nearest supernova in recent years, Supernova 1987a, is also found in the LMC.

## Bridging the gap

Evidence of tidal interaction existing between the galaxies is a bridge of gas that connects SMC with the LMC. A common envelope of neutral hydrogen indicates that the Magellanic Clouds have been bound by gravity for long periods of time. This bridge of gas is a star-forming site.

**FUN FACT**

The most massive star in the universe is thought to be R136a1, located in the LMC.

# Small Magellanic Cloud

The Small Magellanic Cloud (SMC) is an irregular-type galaxy that is roughly 200,000 light years from our Milky Way galaxy and is one of its closest neighbours. It is also one of the most distant objects that we can see with the naked eye. It forms a pair with the LMC and together these are known as the Magellanic Clouds. They were named after the navigator Ferdinand Magellan.

*SMC is located in the constellation of Tucana and appears as a hazy, light patch in the night sky.*

## Mini Magellanic Cloud (MMC)

Speculations exist that the SMC could be split in two, with a smaller portion of this galaxy lying behind the main part of the SMC (when seen from Earth). They are separated by about 30,000 light years. This smaller remnant is the Mini Magellanic Cloud.

The SMC has been detected as a foggy image when seen through the telescope in the lighter patch of the night sky. This cloud is located in the Tucana constellation.

## Formation of the SMC

The SMC, along with the LMC, is classified as an irregular dwarf galaxy, that is, a galaxy with an ill-defined shape, rich in gas and dust. A close study of the Magellanic Clouds indicates that they were both once barred spiral galaxies. It contains a central bar structure. Over time, however, the gravitational interactions with the Milky Way distorted the galaxy, creating an irregular-type galaxy.

## Properties of the SMC

It is approximately 7000 light years in diameter and contains about seven billion solar masses. While it is about half the size of the LMC, it comprises almost as many stars. This means that it has a greater stellar density. But, the rate of formation of stars is currently lower for the SMC. This is probably because it has less free gas than LMC, and therefore had periods of more rapid formation in the past.

**FUN FACT**

In some native stories, the LMC/SMC are camps of an old man and an old woman—with other sky people bringing them food from the river, the Milky Way.

# Barnard's Galaxy

It is a dwarf irregular galaxy about 1.6 million light years away and perhaps one-tenth our galaxy's size. Barnard's galaxy or NGC 6822 lies in the constellation Sagittarius and is a member of the Local Group. It is thus named as it was discovered by E. E. Barnard in 1884, with a six-inch refractor telescope. It is one of the galaxies that is closer to our own. With regard to structure and composition, it is similar to the SMC. It is about 7000 light years in diameter.

## Region of star formation

The reddish nebulae reveal regions of active star formation, where hot, newborn stars heat up nearby gas clouds. The bubble is a nebula with a clutch of massive, hot stars at its centre that is sending waves of matter smashing into the surrounding interstellar material, generating a glowing structure, which looks like a ring from our perspective. Likewise, ripples of heated matter that are sent out by young stars are scattered across Barnard's galaxy.

Irregular dwarf galaxies like Barnard's get their bloblike forms due to close encounters with other galaxies. Gravitational force can significantly change the shapes of the passing or colliding galaxies, pulling and throwing stars, and forming irregularly shaped dwarf galaxies, such as NGC 6822.

## Star clusters in the galaxy

Edwin Hubble, during the 1920s, discovered three star clusters in Barnard's galaxy. His belief was that they were all very old objects like the globular clusters in the Milky Way. However, images taken by the Hubble Space Telescope have shown that the three clusters belong to completely different ages. The stars in the cluster called Hubble VII were formed about 15 billion years ago, and are about the same age as our own galaxy and the universe itself. It seems that our galaxy formed most of its big clusters in the first couple of billion years after the Big Bang. Barnard's galaxy, however, has been generating huge star clusters all along. Hubble X is presently the largest active star formation region in NGC 6822. The nearly circular bright cloud at the core of Hubble-X measures about 110 light years across and contains a central cluster, less than four million years old, of many thousands of young stars.

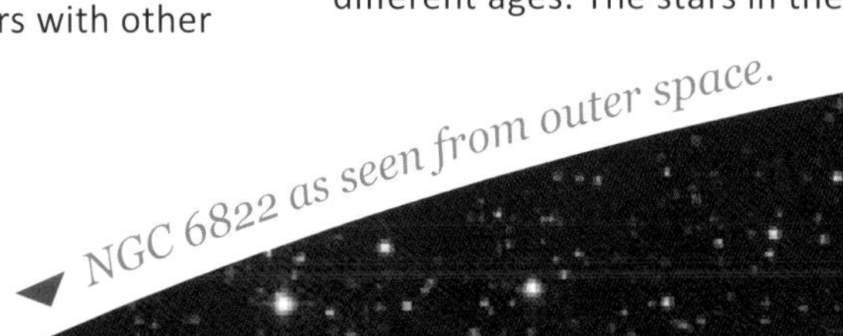

*NGC 6822 as seen from outer space.*

# Sagittarius Dwarf

The Sagittarius Dwarf Elliptical galaxy or Sag DEG, Sgr dE or the Sagittarius Dwarf Spheroidal galaxy, is a small elliptical loop-shaped satellite galaxy of our Milky Way. It lies about 70,000 light years away from Earth in the constellation Sagittarius, while it is currently moving away from us at approximately 140 km per second. It is roughly 10,000 light years across and is home to four known globular clusters, including Messier 54. It had been credited with shaping the Milky Way's spiral arms.

## Orbit around the Milky Way

It has orbited the Milky Way for a period of 550–750 million years about 10 times during its billions of years of existence, at a distance of about 50,000 light years from the galactic centre. During these orbits, it struck our galaxy some 1.9 billion years ago. It then looped over the galactic "north pole" and struck again about 900 million years later. Currently, it is moving back, on course for a third clash with the southern face of the Milky Way disc, which would occur in 10 million years or so.

## How did the Milky Way get its arms?

Sagittarius Dwarf pays a high price though, as it is repeatedly pulled inward by the Milky Way's extreme gravity. It is being ripped apart by the blows, sending huge amounts of its stars and dark matter into the new arms. Its mass at the beginning was about 100 billion times that of our Sun, but has decreased by a factor of two or three. When all that dark matter first collided into the Milky Way, 80–90 per cent of it was detached. That first impact led to instabilities that were enormous, that quickly formed the spiral arms of our galaxy. Impacts among galaxies are believed to be widespread in the cosmos, and many of the spiral galaxies were probably formed in this way.

**FUN FACT**

An amazing theory about how the Sagittarius Dwarf was formed states that it arose from the debris pulled from the LMC after the Magellanic Clouds collided with each other or the Milky Way.

*The Sagittarius Dwarf galaxy as seen from Earth.*

# Sextans A

Sextans A also known as UGCA 205, is a tiny dwarf irregular galaxy. It is about 5000 light years across. With its peculiar square shape, and located 4.3 million light years away from Earth, Sextans A happens to be one of the most distant members of the Local Group. Enormous short-lived stars exploded in supernovae, causing new star formation, producing further supernovae, resulting in an expanding shell. Young, blue stars now highlight areas and shell edges, which appear roughly square to observers from Earth.

*Sextans A as seen from space.*

## Observing Sextans A

Neutral hydrogen gas surrounds several dwarf irregular galaxies. This extends way beyond where the galaxy's starlight weakens. Observations with radio telescopes have confirmed that Sextans A is no exception. What remains an unsolved puzzle is, both, the origin of this hydrogen gas and its effect on the formation of stars. Yutaka Komiyama from Subaru Telescope, with the help of the Suprime-Cam data, is observing Sextans A, and trying to work out a solution.

## Shape and star formation

Irregular galaxies do not have a regular symmetric shape like spiral or elliptical galaxies. These galaxies containing only 100 million to a billion stars are the most common type of irregular galaxy. One main characteristic of such galaxies, besides their shape, is continuous star formation. Sextans A has a mass comparable to only 100 million stars, one-thousandth of the Milky Way. However, it also contains relatively large quantities of dust and gas that are the raw ingredients for stars and planets. In the centre of Sextans A is a high concentration of neutral hydrogen gas that helps new stars develop.

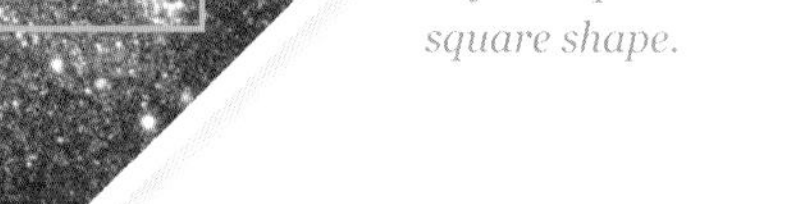

*Sextans A is notable for its peculiar square shape.*

## The mysterious galaxy

When this galaxy was discovered, it created quite a buzz because it had a huge number of stars and also had an odd square shape. What is more mysterious is the fact that it seems like the Sextans was hit by something that set off a reaction of massive short-lived stars. These exploded into supernovae creating more supernovae but the reason for it is still unclear.

### FUN FACT

The bright yellow star that we can see in the image does not belong to the Sextans A at all. This star is a part of our galaxy and can be seen in this image as the picture has been framed in that way.

# Triangulum

The Triangulum galaxy is the third-largest member of the Local Group. It is one of the most distant and permanent objects that can be viewed by the naked eye. It is the smallest spiral galaxy in the Local Group. It is believed to be a satellite of the Andromeda galaxy due to their interactions, velocities and proximity to each other in the night sky.

*This detailed image boasts M33's blue star clusters and pinkish star forming regions that outlines the galaxy's loosely wound spiral arms.*

## Visibility of Triangulum

Under exceptionally good viewing conditions, this galaxy can be seen with the naked eye. Being a spread out object, small quantities of light pollution greatly affect its visibility. The range is between easy visibility through direct vision in very dark skies to using peripheral vision for viewing in rural skies.

## How was it discovered?

It was discovered by Italian astronomer Giovanni Battista Hodierna before 1654. In his work *Desystemate orbis cometici; deque admirandis coeli caracteribus – About the systematics of the cometary orbit, and about the admirable objects of the sky*, he listed it as a cloud-like nebulosity or obscuration and gave the cryptic description, "near the Triangle hinc inde", meaning "a pair of triangles". The galaxy was independently discovered by Charles Messier on the night of 25th–26th August, 1764. It was published in his *Catalog of Nebulae and Star Clusters* as object number 33; hence, the name M33. Triangulum may be home to 40 billion stars, compared to 400 billion for the Milky Way, and one trillion stars for Andromeda.

## Future of Triangulum

The fate of the Triangulum galaxy is unclear, but seems to be linked to its larger neighbour, the Andromeda galaxy. Suggested future scenarios include being torn apart and absorbed by Andromeda, fuelling the latter with hydrogen to form new stars; eventually exhausting all its gas, and thus the ability to form new stars, not permitting it to participate in the collision between the Milky Way and M31, which is most likely to end up orbiting the merger product of the latter two galaxies and fusing with it much later. Two other possibilities are: a collision with the Milky Way before Andromeda arrives or an ejection from the Local Group.

# Nebula

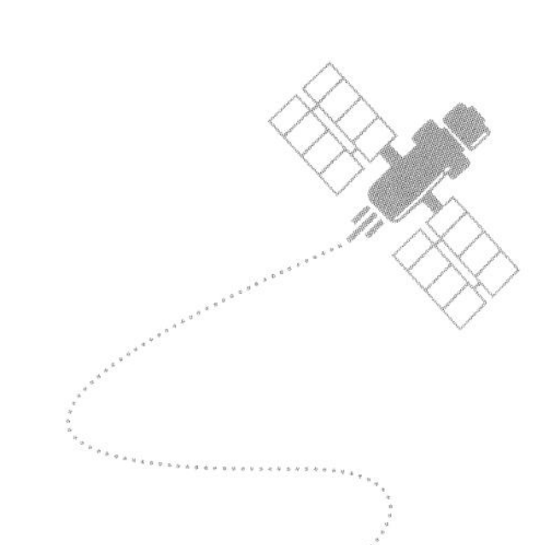

The literal translation of nebula is "cloud". But we know that a nebula is much more than a cloud. What exactly is it? A nebula is an interstellar cloud of dust, hydrogen, helium and other ionised gases. It forms when parts of the interstellar medium coalesce and clump together due to the gravitational attraction of the particles that they are made up of. Nebulae contain the elements from which stars and solar systems are built.

## The nebula cycle

Interestingly, nebulae are not just the starting points of star formation. Ironically, they can also be the end points. This could be thought of as the nebula–star–nebula cycle. Stars that change into red giants could lose their outer layers, also known as atmospheres, as a result of pulsations in these layers. It is this released matter that forms a planetary nebula. One of the four important types of nebulae is the planetary nebula. The others are H II regions, supernova remnant and dark nebula.

## Composition

They show swirls of light. Stars with different elements inside these nebulae cause them to glow with beautiful red, blue and green hues. Most nebulae are composed of approximately 90 per cent hydrogen, 10 per cent helium and 0.1 per cent heavy elements, such as carbon, nitrogen, magnesium, potassium, calcium and iron. Some of the prominent nebulae are the Crab, Eagle, Orion, Pelican, Ring and Rosette Nebulae.

**FUN FACT**

**In 1764, William Herschel mistakenly described the nebulae as "planetary" when he thought that the celestial body at the centre was a planet.**

*Images showing the varied rich colours of Nebulae, like the Crab, Eagle, Orion, Pelican, Ring and Rosette Nebulae.*

# Star Cluster

Many stars tend to gather around each other, drawn by their gravitational fields. These groups of stars are called "star clusters". A globular cluster is one that consists of a spherical collection of stars. These orbit a galactic core. Their spherical shapes and the relatively high stellar densities towards their centres are due to the high gravity that they experience. Globular clusters are fairly common—the Milky Way has around 150–158 of these.

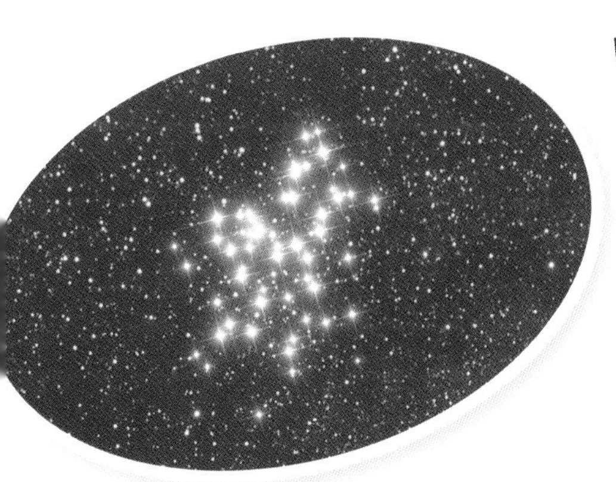

### Butterfly cluster

The Butterfly cluster, also known as Messier 6, or M6, is an open star cluster in the constellation of Scorpius. It gets its name due to its butterfly-like shape.

Giovanni Battista Hodierna was the first to record it in 1654. It is 1600 light years away, 12 light years in diameter and estimated to be 95 million years old. It is best seen during June, July and August from the Southern Hemisphere.

### Pleiades

This star cluster is also known as the "Seven Sisters" and "Messier 45". It is a remarkable object in the night sky with a prominent place in ancient mythology. The cluster contains hundreds of stars, of which only a handful are commonly visible to the naked eye. The stars in the Pleiades were formed together over 100 million years ago, making them 1/50th the age of our Sun. They lie 425 light years away.

### Binary stars

Albireo is located in the constellation Cygnus. It appears as a single point of light to the naked eye, but a telescope shows it to be a binary star. Binary stars are two stars bound together by their mutual gravitational attraction. These stars take thousands of years to orbit around each other. Alberio is 380 light years away. More than half of the existing ones live in binary systems. The Sun is unusual as it is solitary.

### Globular cluster

It is a large group of old stars that are closely packed in a symmetrical manner. They get their name because of their uneven spherical appearance. They are the largest, most massive star clusters. Though several globular clusters are visible to the naked eye as hazy patches of light, they were heeded only after the telescope was invented.

### Close pair

If two stars orbit each other at large distances, they evolve independently and are called a "wide pair". If the two stars are close enough to transfer matter via tidal forces, they are called a "close" or "contact pair". A team of astronomers discovered a close pair of white dwarf stars—tiny, extremely dense stellar remnants—that have a total mass about 1.8 times that of the Sun. When these two stars merge in the future, they will create a thermonuclear explosion leading to a Type Ia supernova.

# Gas and Dust

Stars are born in the densest regions of the interstellar medium, or ISM, called molecular clouds. ISM is the name given to the gas and dust that exists between the stars in a galaxy. It is 99 per cent gas and one per cent dust, by mass. Molecular clouds are perfect star-forming regions, because the combination of these atoms into molecules is possible in very dense regions. Let us take a look at the various star formations that occur in the heavens above.

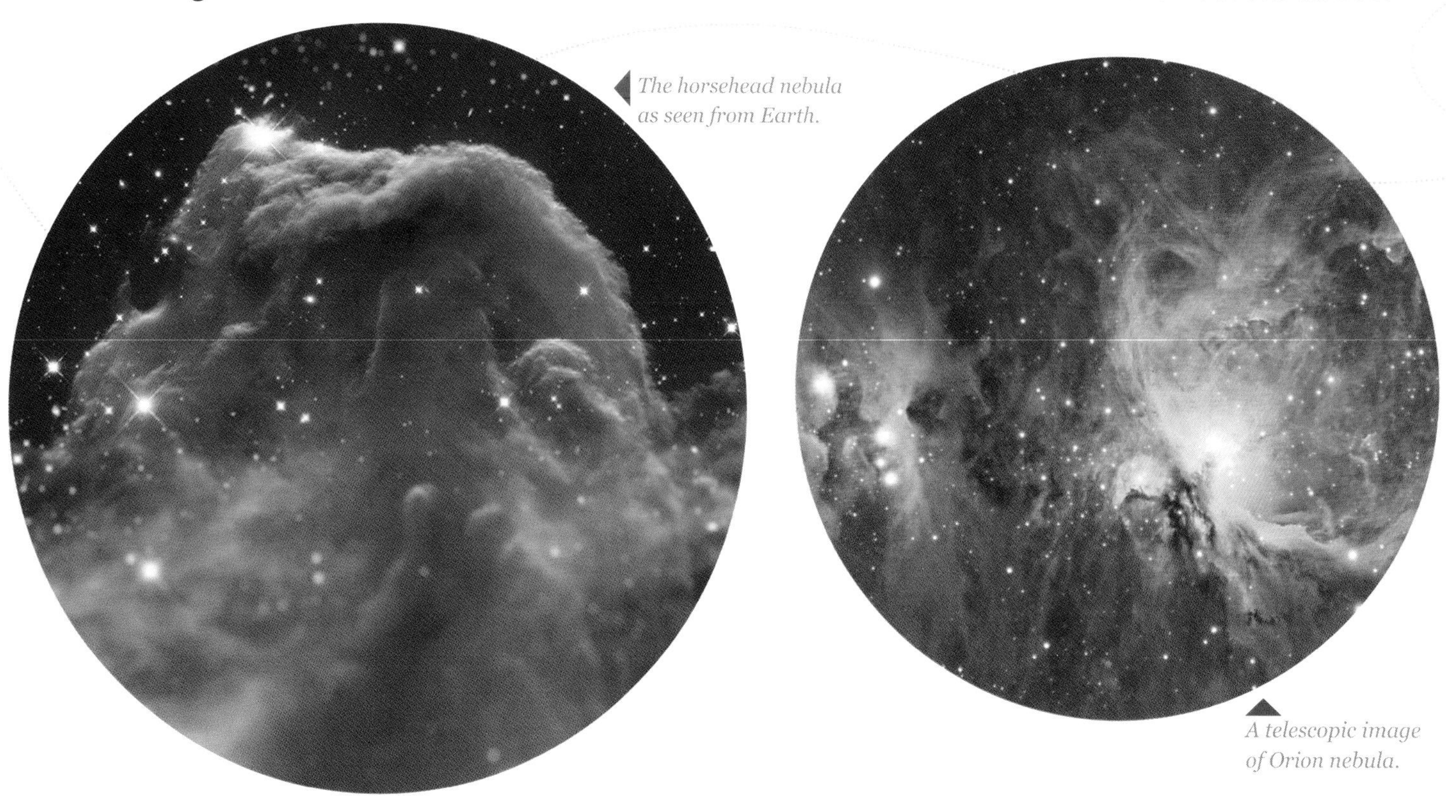

*The horsehead nebula as seen from Earth.*

*A telescopic image of Orion nebula.*

## Horsehead nebula

The horsehead nebula is a dark nebula in the Orion constellation. It is also known as Barnard 33 (B33), as it was first photographed by American astronomer Edward Barnard. The nebula is situated south of the Alnitak star and is a part of the larger Orion molecular cloud complex. The Horsehead Nebula is approximately 1200 light years from Earth.

## It is easily identifiable

It is easily identifiable because of its swirling cloud of dark dust and gases, which bears some resemblance to a horse's head. The pinkish glow is due to hydrogen gas ionised by the Sigma Orionis star that is nearby. The magnetic fields separate the gases, rendering the nebula into glowing streaks.

## Orion nebula

It is the most noticeable of all constellations. The three stars of Orion's belt jump out at you midway between Orion's two brightest stars, Betelgeuse and Rigel, the two brightest stars in the sky. Once you find the belt stars, you can also locate the Orion Nebula, which is also known as M42, a stellar nursery where new stars are born. The higher the constellation Orion is in the sky, the easier it is to see it. It is due south and highest in the sky at midnight during mid-December. The stars return to the same place some four minutes earlier each night, or two hours earlier each month.

## Visibility

Look for Orion to be highest up around 10 pm during mid-January and 8 pm during mid-February. It is around 30–40 light years in diameter, giving birth to perhaps a thousand stars. Within the nebula is seen a young open star cluster. The stars of the cluster were born at the same time from a part of the nebula and are still bound together loosely by gravity. It is sometimes known as Orion nebula star cluster. An international team of astronomers, in 2012, proposed that this cluster within the Orion nebula may have a black hole at its centre.

*Research from 2007 suggests that a stellar supernova could have already blown the pillars out of formation 6000 years ago. Because light takes time to travel, it may be another thousand years before we can see the end of these pillars.*

*The ETA Carina Nebula NGC 3372.*

## Pillars of creation

One of the images taken by Jeff Hester and Paul Scowen using the Hubble Space Telescope in 1995 became famous as the "Pillars of Creation", depicting a large region of star formation. The small dark areas are believed to be proto-stars. These columns are composed of interstellar hydrogen gas and dust, which act as incubators for new stars. Astronomers have found dense pockets of gas, aptly called "Evaporating Gaseous Globules" (EGGs) at the top of these pillars, where stars are believed to be formed.

## ETA Carina nebula

ETA Carina nebula is also called the Carina Nebula or the Great nebula in Carina, a spectacular diffuse nebula in the constellation Carina. It is one of the largest and brightest in the sky. It is almost 7500 light years away. The ETA Carina nebula or NGC 3372 is one of the largest HII regions in the entire Milky Way.

It is four times larger bigger the Orion nebula, which itself forms a portion of the Orion molecular cloud complex. The only reason that the Carina nebula is not well known is because it cannot be seen from most of the northern hemisphere. It was discovered by Abbé Nicolas Louis de Lacaille during his two-year journey to the Cape of Good Hope during 1751–52. In addition to ETA Carina, the nebula consists of many stars that are some of the hottest and most massive known. Each star is about 10 times as hot and 100 times as huge as the Sun.

## New born star

The IRS 4 is a rare newborn star that is actually around half the age of the human race. It is 100,000 years old, with the surrounding material called Sharpless 2-106. The IRS 4 acts as an emission nebula as it emits light after being ionised, while dust far from IRS 4 reflects light from the central star. Therefore, it acts as a reflection nebula.

**FUN FACT**

As Earth rotates, the stars come back to the same place in the night sky every 23 hours, 56 minutes and 4.09 seconds. This is a sidereal day, or star day.

*IRS 4 is one of the rare stars that is actually younger than the human race.*

# The Sun as a Deity

Across history, like most other natural phenomena, the Sun remains an object of worship in several cultures. Man's basic understanding of the Sun is as a glowing disc in the sky, whose rising above the horizon causes day and whose setting brings on the night. In several pre-historical cultures, the Sun was believed to be a solar deity or some other supernatural phenomenon.

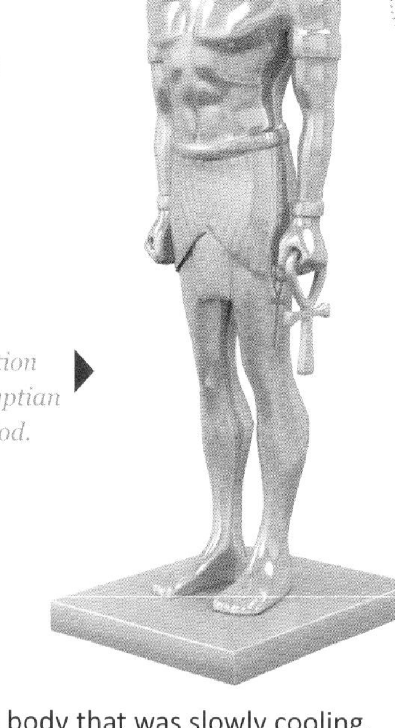

*Depiction of Egyptian Sun God.*

## Importance of the Sun

Worshipping the Sun was central to civilisations, such as the ancient Egyptians, Incas of South America and Aztecs of Mexico. In religions such as Hinduism, the Sun is still considered a deity. The Egyptians portrayed Ra (the Sun) as being carried across the sky in a solar barque, accompanied by lesser gods. To the Greeks, he was Helios, carried by a chariot drawn by fiery horses. From the reign of Elagabalus in the late Roman Empire, the Sun's birthday was a holiday celebrated as Sol Invictus, meaning "unconquered sun".

## Growth of scientific understanding

Greek Philosopher Anaxagoras was one of the first to scientifically and philosophically explain about the Sun. He suggested that the Sun was a giant flaming ball of metal. The moon according to him, reflected the light of the Sun.

## The Sun is the centre of our galaxy

During the third century BCE, Aristarchus of Samos, Ancient Greece, first proposed the theory that the Sun is the centre around which the planets move. During the early years of the modern scientific era, the source of the Sun's energy was a significant puzzle. Lord Kelvin proposed that the Sun was a liquid body that was slowly cooling. And that, it radiates an internal store of heat.

**According to Greek mythology, Helios, a solar deity, was a charioteer who drove his fiery vehicle through heaven by day. During the night, he floated back across the ocean in a golden bowl, to mount his chariot again the next morning.**

*Solar system with the Sun, planets and stars.*

# Our Galaxy

▲ *Earth and our galaxy. This image shows Earth at night with trillions of stars that form our galaxy.*

A galaxy is a massive, gravitationally bound system consisting of stars, stellar remnants and interstellar mediums of gas, dust and dark matter. The word "galaxy" is derived from the Greek word "galaxias", meaning "milky", referring to the Milky Way.

Galaxies contain multiple planets, star systems, star clusters and many types of interstellar clouds. An interstellar medium of gas, dust and cosmic rays, all lie between these objects. Many galaxies are believed to have supermassive black holes at their centre.

There are more than 170 billion galaxies in the universe. Most are 1,000–100,000 parsecs in diameter. The majority of the galaxies are organised into galaxy groups and clusters, which in turn usually form larger superclusters. At the largest scale, these associations are arranged into sheets and filaments or even walls that are surrounded by massive voids.

# Types of Galaxies

The current estimate suggests that there are between 100 and 200 billion galaxies in the universe. Each one of these has hundreds of billions of stars. A recent German supercomputer simulation has pegged that number to be even higher than 500 billion. In short, there could be a galaxy out there for every star in the Milky Way. The Hubble Space Telescope is used to explore space and learn more about it. This telescope gives us an estimation of the number of galaxies that actually exist. There are various types of galaxies in the universe.

## Elliptical galaxy

This is the most abundant type of galaxy found in the universe. However, because of their age and dimness, they are outshone by younger, brighter collections of stars. These galaxies do not have the swirling arms of their more well-known siblings, the spiral galaxies. In contrast, they are more rounded and in the shape of an ellipse, a stretched-out circle. Some stellar collections are more stretched than others. Elliptical galaxies are denoted by the letter E. They are also given a number from 0 to 7. An E0 galaxy looks like a circle while an E7 galaxy is elongated and thin. These galaxies have an extensive range of sizes. The largest elliptical galaxies could be more than a million light years in diameter. The smallest or the dwarf elliptical galaxies are less than one-tenth the size of the Milky Way. These galaxies have very little gas and dust.

## Spiral galaxy

Most of the bright galaxies in the neighbourhood of the Milky Way are spiral galaxies, although irregular galaxies are the most common. Spirals have the smallest range of masses and sizes. These objects can contain between 10,000,000,000 and 400,000,000,000 times the mass of our Sun, and their diameters range from 16,300 to 163,000 light years. Our own Milky Way is close to the upper value. All spiral galaxy labels begin with the letter S, followed by a lower case letter a, b or c.

## Barred spiral galaxy

A barred spiral galaxy is one with a bar through the centre. Around two-thirds of the spiral galaxies have a bar-like region of stars at the centre. Their spiral arms emerge from the two ends of the bar that guide gas and dust towards the central bulge. The flow of this matter results in many barred spirals to have active nuclei. New stars are born as a result of gas and dust from these galaxies.

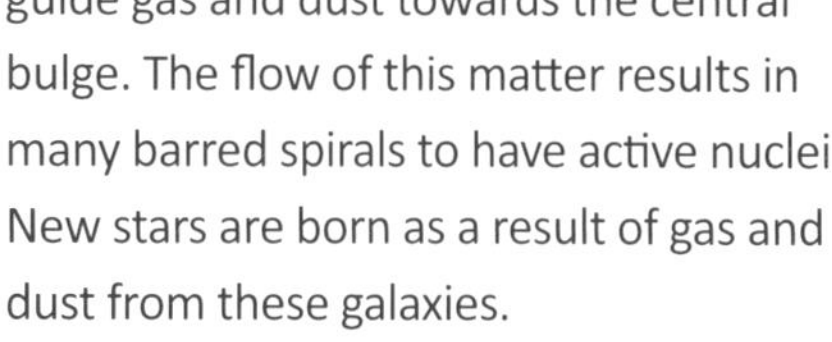

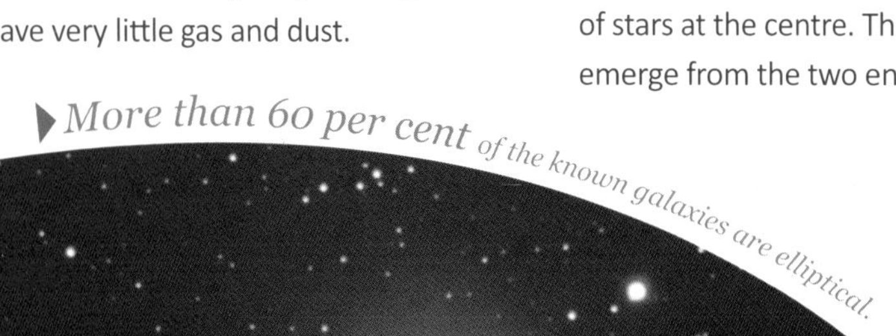

More than 60 per cent of the known galaxies are elliptical.

Messier 109 is a barred spiral galaxy.

Spiral galaxies are named after the spiral shape formed by their stars.

About 20 per cent of all galaxies are irregulars.

Lenticular galaxy in space surrounded by thick dust lanes.

## Lenticular galaxy

Lenticular galaxies share characteristics of both spiral and irregular galaxies. Like spiral galaxies, they have a central bulge and a flat disc-like shape. Like irregular galaxies, they are populated by old stars. The Sombrero galaxy, also called M104 or NGC 4594, is one of these. It is about 28 million light years from our planet in the constellation Virgo. It gets its name because it resembles a Mexican hat—sombrero. The dark dust lane forms the hat's rim and the galaxy's bulging core forms its crown.

## Irregular galaxy

Irregular galaxies do not have many common features. Many of them are the result of galaxy collisions or near misses. One example of an irregular galaxy is the "starburst galaxy". Starburst galaxies are extremely bright as many new stars are born within a short period. These galaxies are usually found in groups or clusters, where collisions and near-misses between galaxies are common. In case of a few irregular galaxies, the astronomers cannot figure out why they look so strange. These galaxies are denoted by the letters Irr.

# Elements of our Galaxy

A galaxy is an extensive collection of stars, glowing nebulae, gas and dust united by gravity. Scientists believe that a black hole, which is the remains of a massive star, is situated at the centre of many galaxies. The galaxy that contains our solar system is called the Milky Way. There are several elements that form our galaxy.

## Galaxy dust

The space between the stars is filled with gas and tiny pieces of solid particles or dust. Most of this gas and dust result from the death of stars, which either exploded or blew off their outer layers, returning their material to space. From this material, new stars are born. Mostly, this gas and dust can be detected using infrared light.

*Dust usually obscures the view of the stars and the planets.*

## Spiral arms

The Milky Way has spiral arms coming out of its central bulge. These arms are made up of young, bright, blue stars and older, white stars as well as dust and gas. There are stars that lie between these spiral arms; however, they are not as bright. These stars slowly orbit the central bulge following their own path. They take several hundred million years to complete their orbit.

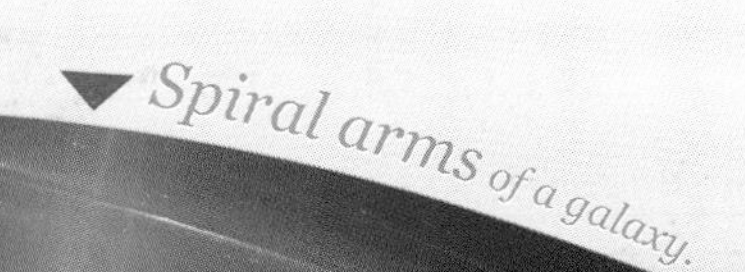

*Spiral arms of a galaxy.*

## Star nursery

Stars are formed within clouds of hydrogen gas. A part of the cloud then forms a dense ball of gas. More gas is attracted because of gravity, thereby compressing the ball into a tighter and hotter mass. As a result, a nuclear fusion is triggered, which converts hydrogen into helium and radiates energy as a very bright star.

*An image of the well-known Carina nebula caught by a European telescope, unveiling the previously hidden features of an exquisite star nursery.*

## Hot blue star

Stars get their colour depending on their temperature. The coolest stars appear red, while the hottest ones are blue. For a star, its temperature is determined by its mass. Blue stars have at least three times the mass of the Sun or even more. Interestingly, whether a star has 10 times the mass of the Sun or 150 solar masses, it appears blue to our eyes.

*Stars display different colours in space. They get their colours due to their temperature and mass.*

## Solar system

Our solar system was formed about 4.6 billion years ago. It includes the eight planets and their natural satellites, dwarf planets such as Pluto and Ceres, asteroids, comets and meteoroids. The Sun contains almost all the mass present in the solar system and exerts a tremendous gravitational pull on the celestial bodies.

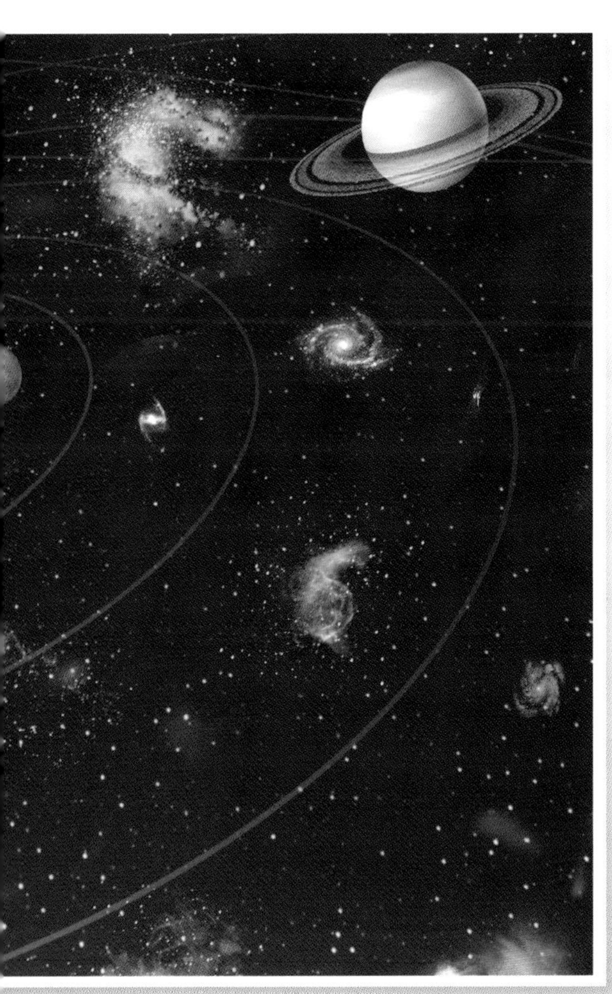

*The Solar System*

## Central bulge

A galaxy contains stars, gas and dust. In a spiral galaxy such as the Milky Way, the stars, gas and dust are organised into a "bulge" and "disc", containing "spiral arms" and a "halo". The bulge is a round structure primarily made of old stars, gas and dust. The outer parts of the bulge are difficult to distinguish from the halo. The bulge of the Milky Way is roughly 10,000 light years across.

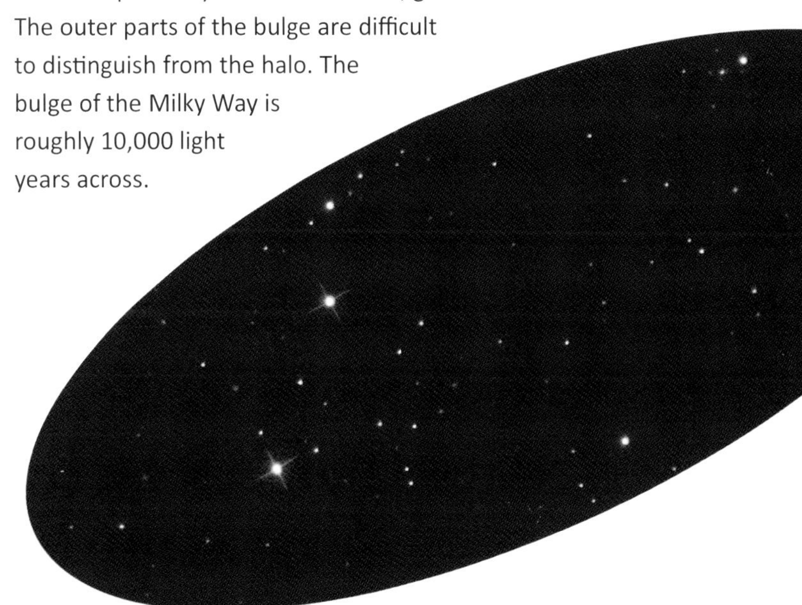

## Black hole

Black holes are huge but surprisingly cover only a small region. Because of their mass, they have an extremely powerful gravitational force. Nothing can escape them; even light is trapped by a black hole. Black holes consist of three parts: the outer event horizon, inner event horizon and the singularity. The event horizon is a boundary around the mouth of the black hole from where light loses its ability to escape. The singularity lies at the centre of the black hole. It is a one-dimensional point that contains infinite mass in a considerably small space.

*Black hole in one of the Nebulas.*

## Dark matter

Dark matter is a kind of matter that cannot be seen using telescopes. However, it accounts for most of the matter in the universe. The existence and properties of dark matter are inferred from its gravitational effect on visible matter, radiation and the large-scale structure of the universe. Dark matter accounts for 23 per cent of the universe.

# Colliding Galaxies

Several galaxies are members of a group or a cluster. As groups and clusters contain several galaxies that are close together, galaxies tend to collide with each other. In fact, it is said that the Milky Way galaxy is colliding with the Sagittarius Dwarf galaxy right now. Galaxy collisions are common, but stars in each galaxy are so far apart that star collisions are extremely rare. Even if galaxies do not actually collide, they can still cause harm to each other.

## When galaxies interact

When two galaxies pass close to each other, the gravity that they exert can cause both of them to bend out of shape. Both crashes and near misses between the galaxies are referred to as "interactions".

## What happens when they collide?

When two galaxies interact, the clouds of gas within each galaxy may compress. Compressing the clouds can cause them to collapse under their own gravity, changing them into stars. This process can lead to a burst of star formation in the interacting galaxies. A new generation of stars may form in a galaxy where the normal star formation may have stopped long ago. Galaxy collisions takes place over hundreds of millions of years, so we cannot see them occur. The various types of galaxies are given as follows:

## Cartwheel galaxy

The cartwheel galaxy is also known as "ESO 350-4". This galaxy is a lenticular and ring galaxy. It is about 500 million light years away in the constellation of Sculptor. It is an estimated 150,000 light years across. It also has a mass of about 2.9-4.8 × $10^9$ solar masses. Scientists have observed that it rotates at 217 km per second. It was discovered in 1941 by a Swiss astronomer, Fritz Zwicky. Zwicky considered his discovery to be "one of the most complicated structures awaiting its explanation on the basis of stellar dynamics". It is slightly larger than the Milky Way.

## Black Eye galaxy

The Black Eye galaxy, also known as Messier 64 (M64), Evil Eye galaxy or Sleeping Beauty galaxy, is a famous spiral galaxy that is located in the constellation Coma Berenices. It lies at a distance of 24 million light years from Earth. It is known for the huge light-absorbing dust band present in front of its central region. This is how the galaxy got its names "black eye" and "evil eye". Because of the dust band, the stars in the galaxy's bright core are blurry. This galaxy is a popular target for amateur astronomers because its bright nucleus can be observed even through a small telescope. Messier 64 is also notable for being composed of two counter-rotating discs, almost equal in mass. The inner disc contains spectacular dust clouds and lanes.

Cartwheel galaxy.

Messier 64 (M64) or the Black eye galaxy.

Mice galaxies right before their collision.

All the stars in this galaxy rotate in the same direction as the gas in M64's core region, that is clockwise, while the gas in the outer regions rotates in an anti-clockwise direction.

## Mice galaxies

These galaxies, which are also known as NGC 4676, are a pair of interacting galaxies that are located around 300 million light years away towards the constellation Coma Berenices. These galaxies get their name because the long streams of stars, gas and dust thrown off of each other as a result of their interaction resemble the tails of a pair of mice. These galaxies will eventually merge to form a single galaxy. The tails are the remains of their spiral arms.

## ARP 272

ARP 272 is a pair of colliding galaxies, which consists of two spiral galaxies, NGC 6050 and IC 1179. It is around 450 million light years from Earth in the constellation Hercules. The galaxies are a part of the Hercules Cluster, which is a part of the Great Wall—one of the largest known structures in our universe. The two galaxies in ARP 272 are in physical contact through their spiral arms.

## Antennae galaxies

The Antennae Galaxies, are a pair of interacting galaxies within the constellation Corvus. Also called NGC 4038/NGC 4039, they are presently said to be passing through a starburst phase. Here, the collision of clouds of gas and dust, with knotted magnetic fields, causes rapid star formation. They were discovered in 1785 by William Herschel. These galaxies are locked in a fatal embrace. They were at one time normal and peaceful spiral galaxies, like the Milky Way, but have spent the past few hundred million years clashing with each other. This clash is so fierce that stars have been ripped from their host galaxies to form a streaming arc between the two. In wide-field images of these galaxies, the reason behind their name is clarified—far-flung stars and streamers of gas stretch into space, which create long tidal tails suggestive of antennae. These two galaxies are known as the Antennae Galaxies because the two long tails of the stars, gas and dust ejected from them due to the collision resemble an insect's antennae. The nuclei of these two galaxies will eventually join to become one giant galaxy.

## UGC 8335

UGC 8335 is an interacting pair of spiral galaxies that resembles two ice skaters. It is located in the constellation of Ursa Major, the Great Bear, around 400 million light years from Earth. The interaction has united the galaxies through a bridge of material and has pulled together two curved tails of gas and stars from the outer parts of their bodies. Both galaxies show dust lanes in their centres. It ranks 238th in the Arp's Atlas of Peculiar Galaxies.

**FUN FACT**

Did you know that the Sun travels around a galaxy once every 200 million years — a journey of 100,000 light years?

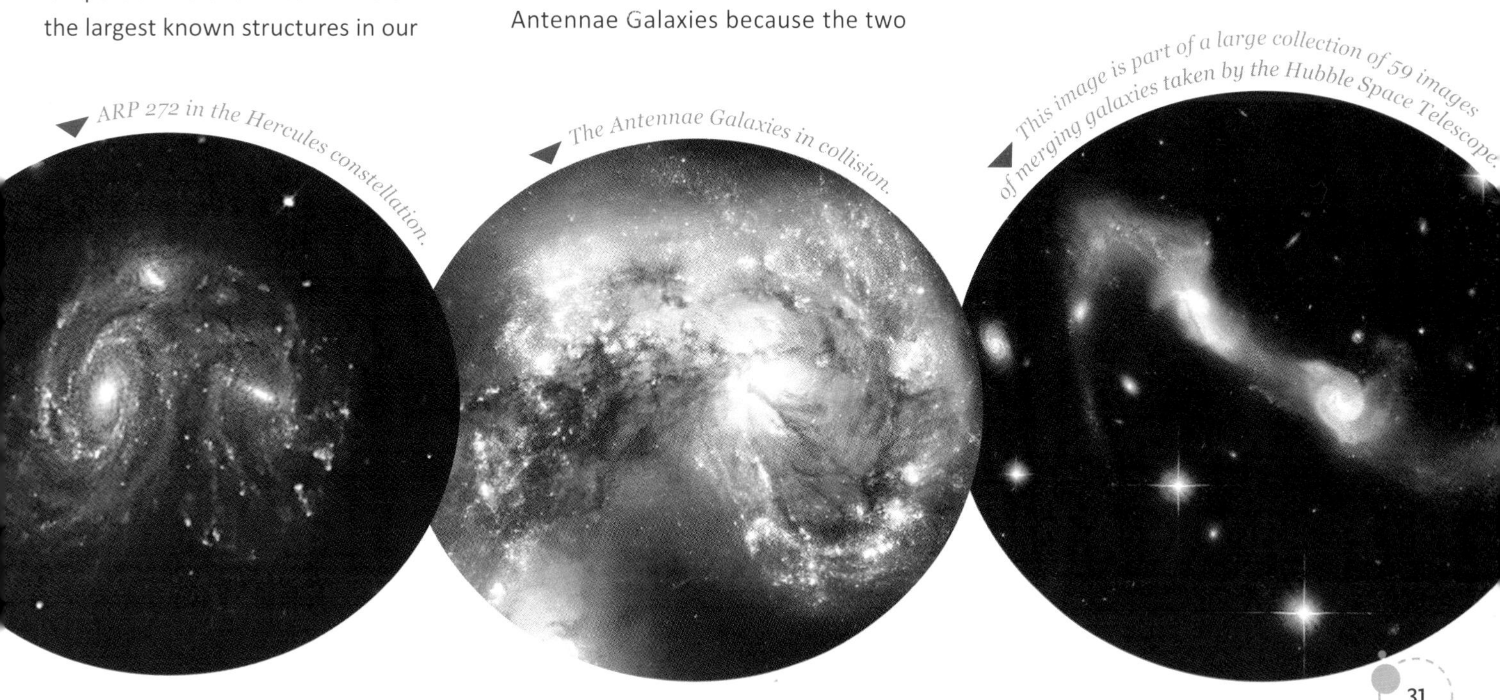

ARP 272 in the Hercules constellation.

The Antennae Galaxies in collision.

This image is part of a large collection of 59 images of merging galaxies taken by the Hubble Space Telescope.

# Active Galaxies

In a normal galaxy, most of the light is emitted from the stars that are evenly distributed throughout the galaxy. However, there are some galaxies that emit intense light from their nuclei (the centre). These galaxies when viewed in the X-ray, ultraviolet, infrared and radio wavelengths, seem to be giving off significant amounts of energy from their nucleus. Such galaxies are called active galaxies. They represent a very small percentage of all galaxies. There are four main types of active galaxies, which are given as follows:

*3C 454.3 is one of the brightest gamma ray sources in the sky. It appears in Pegasus, near Alpha Pegasi.*

## Radio galaxy

A radio galaxy serves as a strong source of electromagnetic radiation or radio waves. Their discovery provides proof that the universe can expand, contradicting the steady state theory, suggesting that the universe would remain steady. Compared to ordinary galaxies, a radio galaxy emits as much as a thousand to a million times more energy per unit time. The giant elliptical galaxy M87 in the Virgo cluster is an example of a known source of radio energy.

## Quasar

Quasars are the farthest objects that can be seen from our galaxy, and are extremely bright masses of energy and light. Quasar is short for "quasi-stellar radio source" or "quasi-stellar object". They are the brightest objects in our universe, although when seen through a telescope they do not appear that bright. This is because quasars are extremely far away. They emit radio waves, X-rays and light waves. They appear as faint red stars to us. Some are believed to produce 10–100 times more energy than our entire galaxy and is only as big as our solar system.

## Blazar

A blazar is a dense energy source fuelled by supermassive black holes. They are considered to be one of the most energetic phenomena in space. These extragalactic objects were first seen and discovered around 1972, because of the technology of "A Very Long Baseline Interferometry". The name was coined by astronomer Ed Spiegel in 1978. They are usually divided into two, the BL Lacertae objects (BL Lac) and Optically Violent Variable (OVV) quasars. There are also a few intermediate blazars, which have the properties of both the BL Lac and the OVV. They are said to emit high-energy plasma jets almost as quick as the speed of light. They are a type of compact quasars.

They are characterised by their high speed and energy. They are also extremely powerful.

## Seyfert galaxy

Almost all Seyfert galaxies are spiral galaxies and are named after the American astronomer Carl Seyfert, who identified them in 1943. They are among the most intensively studied objects in astronomy because they are thought to be nearby, low-luminosity versions of the same phenomenon as observed in quasars. They have cores that emit as much energy at all wavelengths as the total radiation output of our own Milky Way. However, they do not contain well-defined radio lobes. A striking feature of these galaxies is that their luminosity can change rapidly. In the constellation Pegasus, NGC 7742 is known to be a Seyfert galaxy. It is about 72 million light years away. It resembles a fried egg, with a very bright nucleus that is visible at all wavelengths. It is ringed by blue-tinted stars forming regions and faintly visible spiral arms. The yolk—its yellow centre is about 3,000 light years across.

*The power of a quasar originates from supermassive black holes which are believed to exist at the core of all galaxies.*